Sports History

The Story
of Soccer

Anastasia Suen

Published in 2002 by The Rosen Publishing Group, Inc.
29 East 21st Street, New York, NY 10010

First Edition

Book Design: Christopher Logan

Photo Credits: Cover, pp. 5–7, 11 © Bettman/Corbis; pp. 8–9
© Historical Picture Archive/Corbis; p. 10 © Corbis; pp. 12, 15, 18
© Reuters NewMedia Inc./Corbis; p. 13 © Hulton-Deutsch Collection/Corbis; pp.
17, 20–21 © Duomo/Corbis; p. 19 © AFP/Corbis; p. 20 (inset)
© Wally McNamee/Corbis.

Suen, Anastasia.
The story of soccer / by Anastasia Suen.
    p. cm. — (Sports history)
Includes bibliographical references and index.
ISBN 0-8239-5998-8 (lib. bdg.)
1. Soccer—Juvenile literature. [1. Soccer—History.] I. Title.
GV943.25 .S92 2001
796.334—dc21
                                        2001000649

Manufactured in the United States of America

Contents

The First Kicking Games

Kicking games using a ball have been played for many thousands of years. People all over the world have played these kinds of games. The ancient Chinese, Greeks, Mayans, and Egyptians were some of the first players.

This ancient Roman artwork shows a man and child playing a ball-kicking game.

Football in England

By the 1800s, one kind of ball-kicking game was very popular in England. Students at English schools liked to play it. This game became known as football.

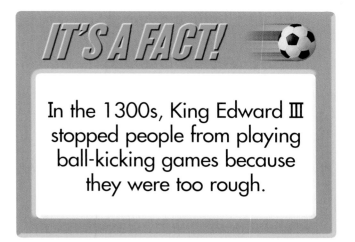

In the 1300s, King Edward III stopped people from playing ball-kicking games because they were too rough.

7

Football rules were different from city to city. In 1863, a group of 11 teams created a set of rules for everyone to follow. The group was called the Football Association.

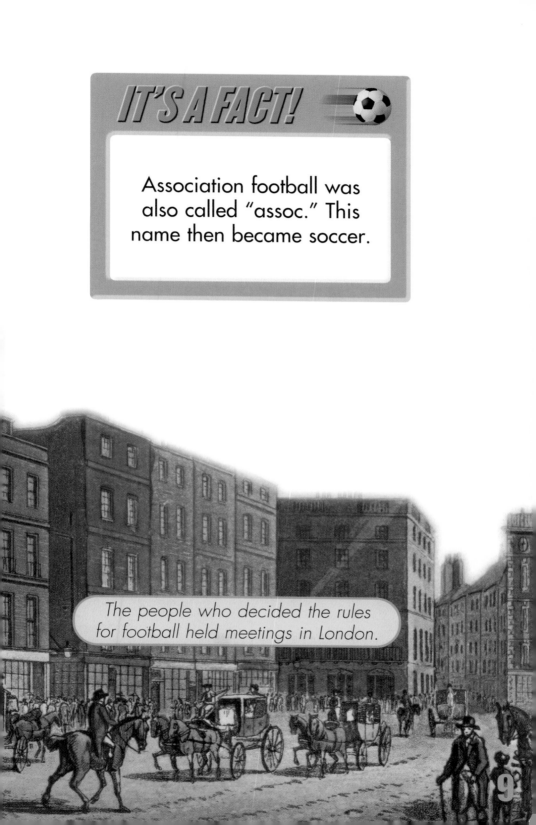

Association football was also called "assoc." This name then became soccer.

The people who decided the rules for football held meetings in London.

Soccer Around the World

Traveling British sailors brought soccer to people around the world. Soccer associations began all over Europe and as far away as South America.

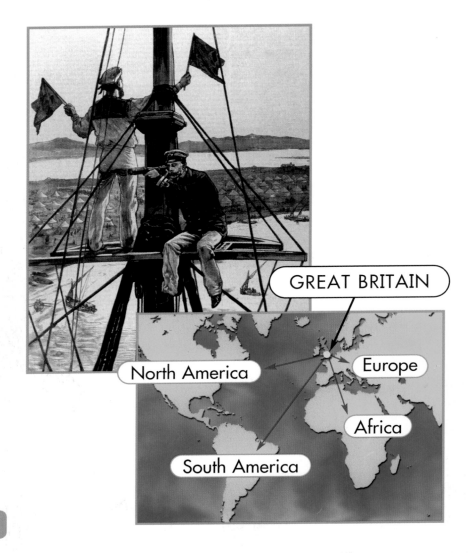

GREAT BRITAIN

North America

Europe

Africa

South America

The Fédération Internationale de Football Association (FIFA) was established in 1904 to organize all of the national soccer associations in the world.

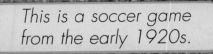

This is a soccer game from the early 1920s.

In 1930, the first world championship games were held. These games were called the World Cup.

Winners of the World Cup trophy keep it until the next games are held.

Teams from 13 countries played against each other. The first World Cup was won by Uruguay. The World Cup is held every four years.

WORLD CUP 1938

This is the start of the 1938 World Cup final game between Italy and Hungary.

Today, 32 countries can play in the World Cup. It takes almost two years of playing to choose the 32 best teams from around the world.

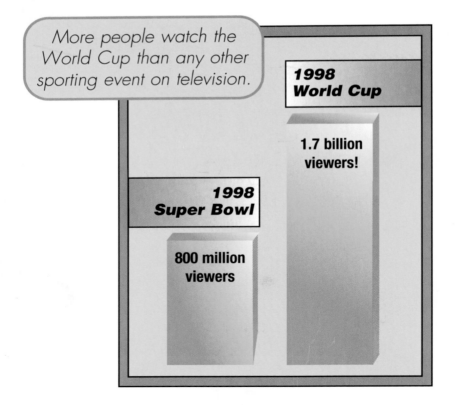

More people watch the World Cup than any other sporting event on television.

1998 World Cup

1.7 billion viewers!

1998 Super Bowl

800 million viewers

Olympic Soccer

Soccer has been an Olympic sport since 1900. Winning an Olympic gold medal is hard because soccer is played in so many countries. Only Great Britain and Hungary have won as many as three gold medals.

The United States played China in the 2000 Summer Olympic Games.

Women and Soccer

Women have played soccer for many years. In 1991, the United States women's team won the first Women's World Cup.

The United States women's team also won the 1999 Women's World Cup.

In 1996, the United States women's team won the first women's Olympic soccer gold medal.

Mia Hamm (right) tries hard to get the ball in the 2000 Olympics.

In Brazil, a record-breaking 199,854 people once attended a soccer game! This was the largest number of people to ever attend a sporting event.

Pelé is one of the greatest soccer players of all time.

Soccer is played in more than 200 countries. There are hundreds of school teams and professional teams. Soccer has become the most popular sport in the world.

Glossary

association (uh-soh-see-**ay**-shun) an organized
    group

championship (**cham**-pea-uhn-shihp) the last
    game of a sport's season that decides which
    team is best

national (**nash**-uh-nuhl) having to do with an
    entire country

professional (pruh-**fehsh**-uh-nuhl) an athlete who
    earns money playing a sport

World Cup (**werld kuhp**) a competition held
    every four years to decide the best soccer
    team in the world

Resources

Books
Soccer
by Ivor Baddiel
Dorling Kindersley Publishing (1998)

Kids' Book of Soccer: Skills, Strategies, and the Rules of the Game
by Brooks Clark
Carol Publishing Group (1997)

Web Site
All About Soccer
http://members.aol.com/msdaizy/sports/
    soccer.html

Index

Word Count: 356

Note to Librarians, Teachers, and Parents

If reading is a challenge, Reading Power is a solution! Reading Power is perfect for readers who want high-interest subject matter at an accessible reading level. These fact-filled, photo-illustrated books are designed for readers who want straightforward vocabulary, engaging topics, and a manageable reading experience. With clear picture/text correspondence, leveled Reading Power books put the reader in charge. Now readers have the power to get the information they want and the skills they need in a user-friendly format.